The Complete Guide to Connecticut Divorce

by Attorney Theresa Rose DeGray
Attorney Jill Ruane

Edited by Jennifer Sanfilippo

 Printed in the United States of America
Different Middle Initial, LLC
ISBN: 978-0-9965631-8-5

Table of Contents

Introduction

If this book caught your attention, it is probably because you are facing a divorce in the state of Connecticut. If you are facing a divorce in another state, some of this information may apply to you, but laws differ from state to state and this book speaks to Connecticut laws only. If you live somewhere outside of Connecticut, I suggest that you contact a divorce lawyer in your state. Please note that every case is slightly different and this book is not intended to provide advice regarding your specific case.

I'm writing this book for you. Yes, YOU. This book is for the mother of two who just found out that her husband is cheating on her. This book is for the guy who comes home after a long day of work and is blindsided by divorce papers. This is for the stay-at-home dad that doesn't know how he's going to make it on his own now that his wife has decided to move on with her life. This book is for the couple that is uncertain if they should attempt mediation instead of litigation, and what the differences are.

In my career working with family law, I've come across cases like these and countless others. You might feel like no one can understand what you are going through. You might feel like you have nowhere to turn. I am here to tell you that these thoughts are not true!

While seeking out this book, you've probably realized that there are a lot of resources out there for people looking for divorce information. No matter what your personal situation is, this book will give you the answers that you are searching for and more. I want to congratulate you on pursuing the tools that you need in order to succeed in divorce - it will make the process much easier. Now, let's get started!

CHAPTER 1:

Introduction To Divorce

Traditionally, there are two different types of divorce cases that you can file. These types are "at fault" and "no fault" divorce. In the past, people needed a reason to get divorced and they had to prove the reason or else the divorce would not (could not) be granted. One spouse needed to be "at fault" for the divorce - hence the term "at fault divorce". Connecticut, like many other states, used to go by this rule. If a person wanted to get divorced, they needed to prove that their spouse was at fault for violating their marital vows or that their spouse abused them in some way.

Nowadays, most states have done away with the fault requirement. In the state of Connecticut, divorces are generally filed under the term no fault divorce. This type of divorce is just what it sounds like - it means that no one is "at fault" for the divorce. This means that when you file, the allegations of the complaint indicate that the marriage has broken down irretrievably, however it does not have to list the specific causes as to why the marriage is being dissolved. This is known commonly as "irreconcilable differences". You won't have to prove any type of abuse or other issue in court when you file for a no fault divorce.

Even if you and your spouse decide to file a no fault divorce, "the determination of whether a breakdown of a marriage is irretrievable is a question of fact to be determined by the trial court". Eversman v. Eversman, 4 Conn. App. 611, 614, 496 A.2d 210 (1985). The only thing that you have to prove to the state in order to be divorced in Connecticut is that, "there is no hope of reconciliation" (in other words, there is no hope of repairing your relationship). This is different from several years ago when one spouse would claim a fault when filing their dissolution complaint. Some states still allow for filing a dissolution based on "fault".

Do not let the allegation of "no fault" confuse you. There are several grounds for divorce which are still brought in throughout the litigation process, as necessary. The law in Connecticut is such that, though you do not have to claim fault in order to be granted a divorce, once the divorce begins, the grounds for divorce can have an impact on the litigation process, such as the division of assets and/or custody. It will be up to your attorney as to when these facts are used in the dissolution, if they are used at all.

Common grounds for divorce include:

- The parties have lived apart by reason of incompatibility for a continuous period of at least the eighteen months immediately prior to the service of the complaint and that there is no reasonable prospect that they will be reconciled;
- Adultery;
- Fraudulent contract;
- Willful desertion for one year with total neglect of duty;
- Seven years' absence, during all of which period the absent party has not been heard from;
- Habitual intemperance;
- Intolerable cruelty;
- Sentence to imprisonment for life or the commission of any infamous crime involving a violation of conjugal duty and punishable by imprisonment for a period in excess of one year;
- Legal confinement in a hospital or hospitals or other similar institution or institutions, because of mental illness, for at least an accumulated period totaling five years within the period of six years next preceding the date of the complaint. CONN. GEN. STAT. § 46b-40(c) (2011).

If you've been contemplating divorce for some time, you want to be completely confident in your decision BEFORE you file for divorce. You should be emotionally ready and have made the emotional break before proceeding. To accomplish this, it is important to seriously consider what divorce will mean for you and your family, and if it is truly the right decision for you. To help you reflect on your relationship with your spouse and determine if your relationship is truly over, consider the following questions.

What Is The Source Of Your Unhappiness?

If you are contemplating getting a divorce, chances are that you are unhappy in your marriage. However, it is important to identify the *reason* why you are unhappy. Does your unhappiness stem from a lack of intimacy with your spouse? If this is the case, divorce may not necessarily be the right step to take – instead, you and your spouse can work on developing a stronger bond and creating a more equal partnership. However, if you are unhappy due to abuse, infidelity, constant fighting, or a lack of commitment to the marriage, divorce might be the right choice for you.

What Will The Consequences Of Your Divorce Be?

In some cases, divorce can be messy. Consider what divorce will mean for your children, your spouse, and the rest of your family. Do you think that you will be better off in the long run, or is divorce an option you are considering just to make you temporarily happier? If you don't feel prepared for a change in finances, income, housing arrangements, custody arrangements, etc., then you should not file for a divorce. Plan ahead, accept the difficulties that divorce can bring, and if you still wish to proceed with your divorce, you know that it is the right decision for you.

Is Divorce A Threat?

In marital arguments, divorce is oftentimes threatened. If you find yourself threatening divorce in the heat of the moment, this is clearly an emotional reaction to a disagreement, and not something that you have rationally thought through. Divorce should be based on a lot of thought and planning, not something that you casually throw out in the middle of an argument. If you find yourself threatening divorce while fighting with your spouse, you probably haven't thought it through yet and should take some time to reflect before making any more plans.

Can You Be Mature About Divorce?

The way that you view your divorce will impact the divorce process and your life after divorce. Many people go into a divorce feeling bitter, resentful, and vengeful. If this happens, prepare for a difficult divorce. If you have children with your spouse and you share custody, your post-divorce life will be extremely difficult if you cannot let go of your anger.

On the other hand, if you can view your divorce in a rational way and refrain from blaming your spouse, the entire process will be much easier, as this will allow you to communicate with and respect your spouse even after the divorce is final. For your own emotional and physical well-being, coming to an understanding with your spouse regarding your divorce and letting go of resentment will be important.

Divorce is an important decision that you should take seriously. Finding the root of your desire to get a divorce will help you understand yourself, your relationship with your spouse, and your needs more fully. For this reason, it is important not to rush into a divorce and make sure that it is the right decision for you.

Pre Divorce Tips

The purpose of marriage is to take two separate lives and meld them into one. This makes divorce difficult, and in some cases, seemingly impossible. There are so many things to consider. Finances, child custody, assets, property – the list goes on and on.

You want to make sure that you get what you are entitled to out of the divorce. And your spouse is doing the same thing for them. Most likely, you are going to butt heads, waste time, money, and energy. This section will go over some pre-divorce steps to make the process easier.

In order to save yourself some trouble, keep this in mind; you never want to enter the divorce process unprepared. By the time you file for divorce, you should already have a plan to help you divide your assets and debt. The plan should also help you get back on your feet once the divorce is finalized. You need to start thinking about the legal and financial ramifications of your divorce.

Begin looking into individual health care, because you will need an individual plan once you are no longer married. In addition, you're going to have a ton of paperwork to gather. Paperwork is needed for titles to property (whether owned jointly or independently), titles to vehicles, or real estate. This will help you prove what you own so that you can keep as many of your assets as possible.

Take inventory of your property and consider what you really want to keep in the divorce. Tax information and birth certificates should also be on hand, as they will be necessary once the divorce is filed. In addition, collect bank statements and statements that outline your debt. Only by doing this can you get a clear picture of what debt you owe and what assets you can keep.

At this point, you need to get organized. If you consult a financial planner in the early stages, you can prepare for legal fees, financial concerns, and how you will support yourself once you are single. Open your own bank account so that you can start severing financial ties with your spouse. If you have credit cards in both of your names, cancel them.

You should also begin thinking about how to split up child custody if you have children with your spouse. If you think that your spouse will fight for sole custody of your children, prepare a strong case. Explain why it is in your children's best interest for you to have at least partial custody.

CHAPTER 2:

Factors In Divorce

As stated in the previous chapter, Connecticut law does not require "fault" in order for two parties to enter a divorce. You or your spouse don't necessarily have to do something wrong to cause the marriage to end.

It is important to keep in mind, though, that divorce can be filed due to a specific event that occurred in which one spouse violated their marital vows. If you feel that your spouse caused the breakdown of your marriage and you want to use this as a factor in your divorce, it is important to keep in mind that it will be up to YOU to prove in court that your spouse's actions led to your divorce. Some pros of presenting a factor that led to your divorce include the following:

- If your spouse has issues such as a violent temper or mental illness, it might affect how custody and/or finances are divided in your divorce.
- Financial damages caused by your spouse could impact spousal support.
- Financial damages caused by your spouse could impact your joint asset or debt division.

It is important to also consider the cons of taking this approach. These cons include the following.

Time

Proving that your spouse is the cause of the breakdown of your marriage can make the divorce process longer. It will take time and money to gather evidence, present your case, and then determine how the finding will impact your divorce. This process occurs a lot. When there is a legitimate reason for the breakdown of the marriage, you will want to consult with your attorney to determine how it will affect the outcome of your dissolution.

Open Court

Keep in mind that the proceedings for your divorce case will be open to the public. Aside from your financial affidavits (which are sealed), your court file is available to the public. Court hearings are also public. You might not want to reveal the inner workings of your marriage to the public or your family, especially if the case concerns sensitive matters, such as a cheating spouse or substance abuse issues. Consider the impact that the open proceedings can have on your children, employment, or other family members.

Burden Of Proof

Even if you know that your spouse is responsible for the breakdown of your marriage, proving this in court can be difficult. You will have to gather evidence as proof, which is not always easy or possible, especially if the event that is leading to your divorce happened years ago. The better your records, the easier it is to prove the faults of your spouse. You should make your attorney aware of any documentation you have collected.

You should speak with an attorney to determine if the cause of the breakdown will impact the outcome of the dissolution.

Factors In Divorce

There are several factors under Connecticut law that are known reasons for the breakdown of a marriage. They include:

- The marriage has broken down irretrievably (no fault claimed);
- The parties have lived apart by reason of incompatibility for a continuous period of at least the eighteen months immediately prior to the service of the complaint and that there is no reasonable prospect that they will be reconciled;
- Adultery;

- Fraudulent contract;
- Willful desertion for one year with total neglect of duty;
- Seven years' absence, during all of which period the absent party has not been heard from;
- Habitual intemperance;
- Intolerable cruelty;
- Sentence to imprisonment for life or the commission of any infamous crime involving a violation of conjugal duty and punishable by imprisonment for a period in excess of one year;
- Legal confinement in a hospital or hospitals or other similar institution or institutions, because of mental illness, for at least an accumulated period totaling five years within the period of six years next preceding the date of the complaint. CONN. GEN. STAT. § 46b-40(c) (2011).

Let's look at each of these factors individually.

Irretrievable Breakdown Of Marriage

I covered this factor of divorce in the last chapter. While the irretrievable breakdown of a marriage means that no one is at fault, it is still something that can lead to divorce, which is why it is listed here. Connecticut is a no fault state and this is the most common way to file for divorce. Most divorce filings in Connecticut will claim an irretrievable breakdown of the marriage.

If you are part of a marriage that just isn't working anymore, but you can't pinpoint a specific reason as to why the marriage is breaking down, you might decide that divorce is the right option for you. If this is the case, you should file for divorce on the grounds of an irretrievable breakdown (or "no fault" divorce). It means that the marriage is broken beyond repair. There may have been a cause to the breakdown, but it is your decision if you want to bring the cause into the dissolution process. Speak with your attorney to determine this.

If you are experiencing one or more of the following issues, you should consider filing a no-fault divorce:

- You and your spouse are unhappy and have been so for a significant period of time.
- You and your spouse have tried to repair your marriage (ex. family therapy, couples therapy, spending time together, etc.) but nothing that you have tried has helped.
- You and your spouse were legally separated in an effort to repair your marriage, but it did not work.
- You and your spouse are no longer invested in making your marriage work.

The good thing about divorce based on the breakdown of the marriage is that you don't have to prove that you or your spouse did anything to lead to the failure of your marriage. Likewise, your spouse doesn't have to prove that you are responsible for the end of the marriage. Even if you or your spouse did things wrong in your marriage, it won't affect the case if you decide not to bring it up in the dissolution process. Regardless, your attorney should still be aware of the details of the breakdown of your marriage. Let the attorney advise you specifically as to what information should be presented to the court.

Divorce can be amicable. If the parties are able to reach an agreement, the attorneys will draw up a separation agreement that outlines all of the parties' assets, debts, and issues. You and your spouse will present the court with this separation agreement and any other supporting documentation showing how you have agreed to split your debt, assets, child custody, child support, spousal support, real property etc. Negotiations for these details can be reached outside of court with the help of lawyers, in mediation, in court, or a combination of them all.

Once the paperwork is received by the court, the waiting period for divorce will begin. Pursuant to law, there is a 90 day waiting period. If you are in agreement with your spouse on all issues, at the end of the 90 day period you can enter into a dissolution agreement. If you cannot agree on how to split your assets and child custody, it will take longer.

When the waiting period is over, the parties begin to use the resources of the court to try to reach an agreement. The court will look at the factors that could have led to the dissolution of your marriage, such as debts, affairs, separation, distrust, conflict of personality, conflict of interests, as well as fault factors. This information will assist third parties and the attorneys in reaching a fair and equitable resolution in your case. Cases can last up to a year or more, depending on how many issues are not in agreement and if the parties need a trial to settle outstanding issues.

Separation

One thing that could lead to the irretrievable breakdown of a marriage is separation for a considerable period of time. If you recall, a divorce based on the irretrievable breakdown of a marriage can occur if, "the parties have lived apart by reason of incompatibility for a continuous period prior to the service of the complaint and that there is no reasonable prospect that they will be reconciled…" Conn. Gen. Stat. § 46b-40(c)(2008).

If you and your spouse have been separated, you might want to start thinking about filing for divorce. This will allow you to file for a no-fault divorce, as you will fulfill the requirements for a divorce based on the irretrievable breakdown of the marriage. Or, if you want to file on some other grounds, you may do so.

The fact that you and your spouse have been separated for a significant period of time will show the court that you have tried to work out your problems before rushing into divorce, but that nothing can be done to save your relationship. There is a common misconception that parties have to be separated prior to filing for divorce. This is not true. While it can help your divorce proceedings, separation is not necessary.

There are specific steps to filing for divorce if you and your spouse have been separated and do not have contact with each other. You can still file for divorce if you can't get in contact with your spouse. An attorney can assist you in the proper steps to filing with the court. If you do not know where your spouse resides, you should inform your attorney of your spouse's last known address, if they have ever been in the military, where they work, or other details that could narrow down the location where they currently reside. The court needs proof that you attempted to reach out to your spouse to notify them of the pending dissolution. Your attorney can assist with meeting the court requirements for service in such a case.

Adultery

One common reason why couples get divorced is because one or both parties were unfaithful over the course of their marriage. A person can file a no-fault divorce even when there has been adultery. The cause of the breakdown of the marriage is an element when considering the division of property, alimony, and more.

This would be considered during the negotiation and settling of the case. The habits of a cheating spouse will also be brought out during the final trial. If you think that your spouse has committed adultery, you will have to prove their infidelity in court if you would like to use it as a factor in your divorce.

Adultery is defined as voluntary sexual intercourse with someone other than a person's spouse. However, it is important to keep in mind that some states recognize other acts as forms of adultery. For example, sexual acts that do not end in sexual intercourse can be considered adultery. If you think that your spouse has committed adultery, even if you are not sure if they actually had sexual intercourse with someone else, you should consult a divorce attorney to determine if you have a case.

You can receive compensation in the form of alimony or by being able to keep some of your assets in the divorce. The choices of your spouse can also affect their ability to care for your minor children. Another thing to consider is if the new significant other should be around your minor children or not.

Remember that accusations will not hold up in court without evidence. Accusations must be creditable. Eyewitness accounts, videos, photos, confession, or other direct proof are the best ways to prove that your spouse committed adultery.

If you do not have direct proof, you can build a case on indirect proof or circumstantial evidence. Indirect proof can include love letters, travel records, hotel receipts, etc. If you can prove that your spouse had the means and the desire to commit adultery through indirect proof, it might be enough to convince a judge that adultery did indeed take place.

Fraudulent Contract

If it is found that you entered into your marriage based on a false claim that your spouse made, this can be used as a factor in your divorce. Finding out that your partner told you big lies could affect your marriage. Furthermore, you might not have gotten married in the first place if your spouse did not keep certain information from you.

For example, bigamy could lead to fraudulent contract. If your spouse lied about their marital status and you find out after you are married that they are still legally married to another person, you could seek a divorce or an annulment as a result of this lie.

A fraudulent contract can lead to either divorce or an annulment in Connecticut. This is because fraudulent contract implies that the marriage was based on lies or deceit, in which case an annulment might be filed for. If you want to file for an annulment, you should contact a Connecticut family lawyer.

Willful Desertion

If your spouse has intentionally left you, you can use willful desertion as a part of your argument for getting a divorce. Willful desertion is defined by the state of Connecticut as, "the willful absenting of one party to the marriage contract from the society of the other, coupled with the intention on the part of the absenting party to live apart, in spite of the wish of the other, and not to return to cohabitation". Casale v. Casale, 138 Conn. 490, 492, 86 A.2d 568 (1952).

In order to prove that your spouse is guilty of willful desertion, you will have to prove all of the following elements: "(1) cessation from cohabitation; (2) an intention on the part of the absenting party not to resume it; (3) the absence of the other party's consent; and (4) absence of justification". Gannon v. Gannon, 130 Conn. 449, 450, 35 A.2d 204 (1943).

Just as in a case of adultery, you will have to prove willful desertion in court. If your spouse is absent from these proceedings, they will not be able to defend themselves against the claims that you are making. It is in your best interest to contact a divorce lawyer in order to see if you have a legitimate case. If you do have a case, a lawyer can help you build evidence.

Habitual Intemperance

Habitual intemperance is defined as an alcohol or drug addiction that prevents a person from carrying out their normal life and business for a large portion if not all of the time. Habitual intemperance can damage a marriage by putting stress and burdens on the innocent spouse. It can lead to emotional, physical, or financial strain for the innocent spouse.

In many cases, a spouse will be witness to the drug or alcohol abuse of their spouse, especially if the spouse abusing drugs or alcohol has a serious problem. Habitual intemperance can lead to a spouse's inability to participate in the workforce and fulfill their spousal duties. If this is the case, the drug or alcohol problem will be taken into consideration when dividing property and custody in divorce.

If your spouse has an alcohol or drug problem that prevents them from sustaining a healthy marriage, you might have grounds for divorce. If this is the case with your spouse, you will want to make the court aware of such habits because it could impact your children and their safety. In order to prove habitual intemperance, you must provide evidence and testimony to support your argument. Some common examples of evidence given in habitual intemperance divorce cases are:

- Proof of money spent on drugs or alcohol.
- Reckless behavior due to drugs and alcohol, such as DUIs or other drug related charges.
- Your spouse's inability to find or keep a job due to their condition.

- Statements from family and friends who have seen how your spouse's issues with drugs have affected your marriage can also be useful testimony in court.

Once you prove that your spouse has a drug or alcohol problem, you should go one step farther and prove that your spouse doesn't intend to get help for this issue, or that treatment methods that your spouse tried in the past have not worked. To prove habitual intemperance, you have to prove that your spouse's issues with drugs or alcohol have been a problem for a year or longer and that they are not getting better.

Cruelty

In many states, cruelty is defined as conduct or action taken by your spouse that harms you physically or mentally. If you want to use cruelty in your divorce proceedings as a way to get more property or custody of your children, you have to prove that the cruelty inflicted upon you by your spouse is sustained and severe. This means that you have to prove that the cruelty has lasted for a long period of time and that it has caused you serious damage. You have to prove that the cruelty and abuse are too severe for you to continue your marriage. Many times parties file for a dissolution after a domestic altercation which leads to an arrest or a restraining order.

If you think you are a victim of intolerable cruelty, consider the following actions. If you are a victim of one or more of these examples, you will probably have a case for intolerable cruelty. Cruelty includes:

- Repeated screaming.
- Repeated displays of rage.
- Knowingly giving a spouse a sexually transmitted disease, while the spouse is not aware of the disease.
- Repeated criticism.
- Physical attacks.
- Wrongful accusations (i.e. if your spouse accuses you of adultery).
- Making an affair public.

- Neglect.
- Giving no explanation for staying away from home for long periods of time.
- Indignities.

Much like adultery, intolerable cruelty can be a deciding factor in questions of asset and custody division. If your spouse has abused you, a judge might believe that they could harm your children as well, and you can be awarded custody of your children as a result.

In order to prove intolerable cruelty, consider using the following evidence:

- Doctor's testimony of physical injuries resulting from attacks.
- Photographs of injuries resulting from attacks.
- Eyewitness accounts of attacks.
- Police reports of fights.
- Testimony of family and friends.
- Fear for your life or the life of your child.

While this is not a comprehensive list, it is a good place to start. If you can prove intolerable cruelty in court, it could have an impact on child custody.

If you are not ready to file for divorce but want to protect yourself and your children from the cruelty of your spouse, you can file for a restraining order. You do not have to be divorced or in the process of getting a divorce in order to file for a restraining order. A restraining order is a separate action with the court.

When a person going through a divorce gets arrested, they can also have a protective order brought against them. If you fear your spouse but they have not committed a crime, you may also get a restraining order against them.

Restraining orders are civil orders. They happen through the civil courthouse and have basis in CGS 53a-151. If a restraining order gets granted, the court will issue a temporary order. Also, they will set a date for a hearing not more than two weeks into the future. At that time, the person who asked for the order must establish evidence as to why it should continue. If they fail to make a case, the restraining order will end.

In Connecticut, a temporary restraining order, also known as an ex parte order, is common. A temporary restraining order is a court order designed to provide you and your family members with immediate protection from your abuser. "Ex parte" means that you can get the order without your abuser present in court.

If the judge grants you a temporary restraining order, they will also schedule a hearing within 14 days. Your temporary (ex parte) restraining order will protect you from the time you file for the restraining order until your full court hearing for a long-term order can take place. Your temporary (ex parte) restraining order goes into effect the day that a judge signs it. The accused abuser can get arrested if they disobey the order after receiving notice of it.

If you are in the middle of a divorce, the court may want to hear from the other side. This might happen before giving a restraining order. A permanent restraining order can be issued only after a court hearing. In the court hearing, you and the abuser both have a chance to tell your sides of the story. This helps to stop violent and harassing behavior. Also, it protects you and your family from the abuser. It lasts up to six months, but can get extended.

Protective orders are issued in criminal court at the time of arraignment. There are two types, full or partial. Full protective orders under CGS 54-63c order a person not to have any contact with the victim. Partial orders prohibit a person from doing anything already illegal to a defendant. This includes stalking, harassing, and more. But, it does not prohibit otherwise legal contact.

You can have a judge hear the evidence before a protective order is issued. The case of State v. Fernando A. (2009) sets forth the applicable law. If you don't request the hearing as soon as possible, you might waive your right to contest the court order. This order can significantly impact your life.

Imprisonment For Life

Your marriage vows include the phrase, "for better or for worse," but no one thinks that these vows include marriage with someone who gets arrested. Being married to someone who then gets arrested and has to serve a life prison sentence or another long sentence can put a strain on the relationship. For this reason, if your spouse has been arrested and is currently serving time in jail, you may want to inform the court of this.

Getting a divorce based on the life imprisonment of your spouse is fairly easy. This is because there is documentation to prove your spouse's imprisonment. All that you have to do is present a judge with your spouse's case and show the prison sentence determined as punishment.

Mental Illness

If your spouse has become mentally unstable over the course of your marriage, you can use this as a factor in your dissolution. If your spouse has become mentally incompetent, insane, or ill, many states consider these issues a factor in divorce. In the state of Connecticut, insanity (or confinement in a hospital due to mental illness) can impact a divorce. You can prove your spouse's insanity or mental illness through:

- Medical records.
- Psychiatric records.
- Proof of institutional care.
- Testimony of doctors.
- Testimony of family and friends.

You can also petition to the court to test your spouse for mental illness if it is affecting your marriage. If your spouse is mentally ill, this factor could affect child custody in your divorce.

CHAPTER 3:

Serving Divorce Papers

If you are at the point in your life where you know it is time for you to get divorced, there are certain steps that you must take in order to do so. Here are the steps that you will have to take in Connecticut in order to file for divorce.

1. Decide If You Will Tell Your Spouse

Before you do anything you should consider if you're going to discuss filing for divorce with your spouse. In the state of Connecticut, you don't have to inform your spouse that you are filing for a divorce before the divorce papers are served.

However, you should consider the repercussions of blindsiding your spouse with divorce papers. You might provoke your spouse to become angry by keeping your true feelings from them, which could result in their desire to be vindictive over the course of the divorce. If you and your spouse have children, maintaining a relationship with your spouse for their sake can be difficult if your spouse is hurt by the way you went about getting the divorce.

Talking to your spouse about the divorce before you file and serve the papers is an individual decision and it will depend on your personal situation. If you are looking for advice, you can always contact a divorce lawyer. It does not matter who files for divorce, but the person who ultimately files will be responsible for the cost of the court filing fee and the fee for service of the divorce paperwork on your spouse.

2. Prepare The Necessary Paperwork

There are two forms that you have to fill out in order to begin the divorce process in Connecticut. These forms are the Summons Family

Actions Form (form number JD-FM-3) and the Divorce Complaint/Cross Complaint Form (form number JD-FM-159).

If you and your spouse have children, you will have to fill out an additional form – the Affidavit Concerning Children Form (JD-FM-164). This form tells the court where your children have lived and whom they have lived with for the five years leading up to the divorce. It also outlines prior visitation or custody cases involving your children if there are any.

The Summons Form is the one that your spouse will receive, explaining the divorce proceedings and telling them when to appear in court. The Complaint Form contains information about you and your family and lists the reason why you are seeking a divorce (you can make a no fault claim, or an at fault claim). Attached to the Complaint Form, you should have the Notice of Automatic Orders (JD-FM-158). This form tells your spouse about the orders that go into effect at the start of each Connecticut divorce case.

These orders prevent you and your spouse from taking actions concerning your property or your children without the knowledge and consent of the other spouse. For example, neither of you will be allowed to take your children out-of-state or sell your home without the consent of the other spouse while your divorce is pending.

Filling out this paperwork can be overwhelming and confusing. If you find that you cannot handle the paperwork on your own, it is a good idea to hire a divorce attorney to assist you. Divorce attorneys are familiar with the paperwork involved in filing for a divorce, and they can ensure that you quickly and correctly fill out all of the forms. Because you must serve your spouse with the proper paperwork, it is best that you have your attorney prepare the necessary paperwork so you do not spend more money on making changes or correcting the initial paperwork.

3. File The Paperwork

When you are confident that you have correctly filled out each form, and you are sure that you want to go through with the divorce, you should bring all of the paperwork to the Superior Court Clerk's office. There are several Superior Court Clerk's offices in Connecticut – you should go to the one that serves the district where you live. The clerk's offices in the state of Connecticut are located at:

Ansonia-Milford Judicial District

- 14 West River Street, Milford, CT 06460
  Danbury Judicial District
- 146 White Street, Danbury, CT 06810
  Fairfield Judicial District
- 1061 Main Street, Bridgeport, CT 06604
  Hartford Judicial District
- 90 Washington Street, Hartford, CT 06510
  Litchfield Judicial District
- 80 Doyle Road, Bantam, CT 06750
  Middlesex Judicial District
- 1 Court Street, Middletown, CT 06457
  New Britain Judicial District
- 20 Franklin Square, New Britain, CT 06051
  New Haven Judicial District
- 235 Church Street, New Haven, CT 06510
  Meriden Judicial District
- 54 West Main Street, Meriden, CT 06451
  New London Judicial District
- 112 Broad Street, New London, CT 06320
  1 Courthouse Square, Norwich, CT 06360
- Stamford-Norwalk Judicial District
  123 Hoyt Street, Stamford, CT 06905
- Tolland Judicial District
  20 Park Street, Rockville, CT 06066
- Waterbury Judicial District
  300 Grand Street, Waterbury, CT 06702
- Windham Judicial District
  155 Church Street, Putnam, CT 06260

When you get to the clerk's office, you should hand in all of the paperwork that you have filled out. In addition, there is a filing fee that you should give the clerk. The filing fee is currently $350, but you can get a waiver of fees signed by a judge if you can prove that you cannot afford to pay this fee. To have the fee waived, you need to fill out the Application for Waiver of Fees/Appointment of Counsel Family Form (JD-FM-75).

When you get to the clerk's office, a clerk will help you determine a Return Date, which is the date that the divorce papers have to be served and filed by. Both you and your spouse should be made aware of this date, but you will not have to appear in court on that day. As the clerk will explain, the Return Date should be set for a Tuesday and you must return the served papers at least six days prior to this date. This gives your spouse the proper notification before they have to respond to the divorce papers.

4. Serve Your Spouse

Once you file the paperwork at the clerk's office, you will have to contact a Connecticut State Marshal, as it is a State Marshal who is responsible for serving divorce papers. State Marshals charge a fee to serve divorce papers, but if you have an Application for Waiver of Fees signed, the court will waive this fee. The court can assign a state rate of $50.00 flat for service by a Marshal if you qualify. The Marshal that you hire will fill out a document referred to as the "Return of Service".

This document proves that the Marshal served the divorce papers to the right person. Once the Marshal fills out this document, you will have to mail it or bring it to the clerk's office. When you return to the clerk's office, be sure to bring all of your original paperwork with you.

In the next chapter I'll talk about steps you should take after being served with divorce papers. However, it is important to note that BOTH parties should take these steps at the beginning of a divorce.

CHAPTER 4:

Being Served Divorce Papers

You might be reading this book because your spouse has served you with divorce papers and you need to know the right steps to take. Maybe you saw it coming. Maybe your spouse even sat down with you and told you that they wanted a divorce. But I certainly come across situations where the spouse served with papers was shocked by them and never saw the divorce coming.

Whatever your personal experience with being served is, it is important that you remain calm. Whether you saw the divorce coming or not, you need to begin preparing for the divorce. Chances are that if your spouse is the one that initiated the divorce, they have already begun getting their affairs in order. Now it is time for you to do the same. Here are some steps that you should take after being served with divorce papers.

1. Collect Yourself And Review The Papers

While this is undoubtedly a stressful and emotional time for you, it is important not to let your emotions get out of control. Give yourself some time to process and deal with the prospect of getting a divorce, but try not to fall into a spiral of depression.

You should also refrain from contacting your spouse at a time when your emotions will get the best of you. Yelling at or threatening your spouse will only make this situation worse. If you feel that you need professional help to deal with this event, consider contacting a therapist. Keeping yourself mentally healthy at this time is essential.

Within the first few days of receiving the divorce papers, you should look over the papers and especially note the due date for response. Once you are served papers, you have a finite amount of time to respond to them. Once you know this due date, you can begin planning what you need to do and create a timeline in order to respond to the divorce papers in a timely manner. Read through the papers and note any inaccurate descriptions, questions that you have, and steps that the papers are asking you to take.

2. Consider Your Representation

Responding to divorce papers is just the beginning of a confusing and time-consuming process. You should decide as soon as possible if you want to hire legal representation or try to go through the divorce representing yourself. Both of these are viable options, but you need to make the right decision for yourself.

Keep in mind that in the long run, hiring a divorce attorney will likely save you time, money, and a lot of stress. You will have someone who understands the divorce process walking you through everything step-by-step. If you are unsure if you should hire a lawyer or not, consider setting up meetings with a few different lawyers. During an initial consultation, you can meet an attorney, discuss your case, discuss fees, and get your questions answered. This is a good option if you are on the fence about hiring legal representation.

3. Take Inventory Of Your Assets And Debt

This is an important step to take early on because it will make the rest of the divorce process smoother. Consider which assets you are invested in keeping after the divorce and consider what you would be willing to give up. Document all of the joint and individual debt that you have, as this will be reviewed in the divorce process. You should also locate documents such as birth certificates and tax information because once the divorce is filed, you will have to present these to the court.

You might want to think about canceling joint accounts that you have with your spouse and putting your individual finances in a personal account. Beware, however, that most divorce proceedings come with certain court orders that prohibit unilateral financial decisions like this, so speak to an attorney before you take these steps.

4. Start Preparing For The Divorce

Now is the right time to start making changes to your lifestyle in preparation for divorce. Will this divorce affect your financial situation? Be proactive and start saving some money, looking for a job if you aren't currently working (or a job that pays more money) and make sure that you have good credit if in the future you will be looking for a new apartment or home. Now is also the time to start researching individual healthcare plans. Taking these steps now will ensure that the divorce process and your life after divorce will go as smoothly as possible.

5. Talk To Your Children

If you have kids, it is important that you (and your spouse, if possible) have a straightforward conversation with your children about what is happening. It is extremely common for children to blame themselves when they learn that their parents are getting divorced, so it is important that you directly address these fears. You want to put their anxiety to rest and tell your children that they have done nothing wrong.

It is also important to keep your children in mind throughout this process. Maybe you want full custody of your children, but you have to ask yourself if this is truly right for them or if it is a selfish desire. You might want to badmouth your spouse or fight with them in front of your children, but is that really going to foster a healthy relationship between you and your children, and your children and their other parent? This is not the time to be selfish. As a parent, you need to consider how your actions will affect your children.

CHAPTER 5:

Dividing Assets And Debt

As mentioned in the previous chapter, it is important that you begin taking inventory of your assets and debt as soon as you decide that you will be getting a divorce. This is because splitting up assets and debt can be one of the longest and most frustrating aspects of the divorce process. However, it does not have to be. If you can maintain open communication with your spouse, this process can be painless. Even if you and your spouse cannot divide your assets amongst yourselves, if you are informed about the process, it will make it much easier. To this end, let's take a look at how certain assets and debt are divided in the state of Connecticut in divorce.

Marital Property Vs. Separate Property

There are two different types of property (and debt, for that matter) - marital and separate. Determining who keeps what will hinge on how the property is defined. Marital property is all of the property that you and your spouse acquired over the course of your marriage.

For example, if you and your spouse purchased a house during your marriage, it is considered marital property. If you have a bank account, regardless of the name it is held in, it is marital property. If you bought a fishing boat during the marriage, it is marital property.

The examples could go on and on, but the bottom line is that anything purchased over the course of your marriage belongs to you and your spouse. This means that marital property isn't necessarily property with both you and your spouse's names on it, but property purchased over the course of your marriage.

On the other hand, there is separate property, which refers to assets or debt that you had before you were married. For example, if you bought a car a few years before your marriage took place, that car is your personal property. It belongs to you, which means that in the divorce it would be difficult for your spouse to make a claim to it. But, some separate property can become marital property. This can happen if your spouse contributes to the property. For example, if you bought a home before you were married, but you and your spouse renovated it together, they have some claim to the equity and possibly more. Property division is tricky and I will go into more detail about it later in this chapter.

Another example of an asset that could have begun as separate property and became marital property is a 401k plan. You may need to determine how much was in the account at the time the marriage took place to decide what type of property it is.

It is in your best interest to take an inventory of your assets and debt and determine what is marital property and could be considered separate property. But let's talk about what these terms actually mean in the way that your assets will be divided.

The states of Alaska, Arizona, California, Idaho, Louisiana, Nevada, New Mexico, Texas, Washington, and Wisconsin all follow what is referred to as community property laws in divorce cases. This means that all property is either divided into marital property or separate property. Marital property is considered to be owned equally by both spouses and separate property is considered to be owned by one spouse. In divorce, the marital property is divided equally, and separate property is given to the spouse that it belongs to.

All other states, Connecticut included, use equitable distribution laws. Equitable distribution uses the same definitions of marital and separate property. However, equitable distribution law differs from community property law in that it divides all assets that are accumulated during the marriage in an equitable way. This means that the property will be divided fairly, but this does not mean that property and assets are divided equally.

Equitable distribution law takes into account each party's individual financial situation and earning capacity and divides the property in relation to these factors. For example, if one spouse in the divorce is a stay-at-home mom, and the other spouse is a Chief of Medicine at a prestigious hospital, their individual financial situations will probably be different. Factors such as occupation, earning capacity and education come into play when dividing assets. The wife in this scenario might receive a larger portion of joint assets because her earning capacity is less than her husband's.

Likewise, you and your spouse share the responsibility of the debt that you have accumulated over the course of your marriage. If you have a mortgage on your home, this will have to be divided between the two of you. If you have joint loans or joint tax returns, the debt will be divided between the two of you. Just as with property and asset division, these joint debts accumulated over the course of your marriage will be considered marital debts.

On the other hand, debt that you have from before the marriage took place is your responsibility alone, just as your spouse's separate debt is their responsibility. In the state of Connecticut, debt is divided just as property and assets are – through the equitable distribution laws. Again, several factors are looked at when determining who is responsible for what debt. The court will consider the occupation of the parties, who created the debt, what the debt was created for, and other factors.

Here is the official statute concerning the division of property for the state of Connecticut if you would like to refer to it:

Sec. 46b-81. (Formerly Sec. 46-51). Assignment of property and transfer of title.

(a) At the time of entering a decree annulling or dissolving a marriage or for legal separation pursuant to a complaint under section 46b-45, the Superior Court may assign to either spouse all or any part of the estate of the other spouse. The court may pass title to real property to either party or to a third person or may order the sale of such real property, without any act by either spouse, when in the judgment of the court it is the proper mode to carry the decree into effect.

(b) A conveyance made pursuant to the decree shall vest title in the purchaser, and shall bind all persons entitled to life estates and remainder interests in the same manner as a sale ordered by the court pursuant to the provisions of section 52-500. When the decree is recorded on the land records in the town where the real property is situated, it shall effect the transfer of the title of such real property as if it were a deed of the party or parties.

(c) In fixing the nature and value of the property, if any, to be assigned, the court, after considering all the evidence presented by each party, shall consider the length of the marriage, the causes for the annulment, dissolution of the marriage or legal separation, the age, health, station, occupation, amount and sources of income, earning capacity, vocational skills, education, employability, estate, liabilities and needs of each of the parties and the opportunity of each for future acquisition of capital assets and income. The court shall also consider the contribution of each of the parties in the acquisition, preservation or appreciation in value of their respective estates.

Retirement Funds In Divorce

Determining what you have a right to in your divorce can be difficult. One major asset that you might be concerned about in divorce is your retirement fund. If you are confused about if and how your retirement fund will be divided, the law can clarify certain aspects of dividing this asset.

By law, you are not allowed to divide your retirement assets without being penalized. The only time that you can divide your retirement fund is when you are going through a divorce. This doesn't mean that you or your spouse can liquidate your assets without penalty, but it does allow you to divide your retirement funds if you want to.

In most cases, this is achieved when both parties file a Qualified Domestic Relations Order (QDRO). It is important to keep in mind that this area of the law can be tricky, and the ability to divide your retirement funds and this process will vary based on the company you work for and the parameters of your individual retirement plan. For this reason, every case of dividing retirement funds is different. You will get the best information for your situation by contacting a divorce lawyer.

Filing a QDRO can be a difficult process because these forms need to be filled out in a precise manner. You will have to gather a lot of information about your retirement plan and your spouse's plan in order to fill out this form. In addition, in order to qualify, you have to make sure that your retirement plan is covered by the Employee Retirement Income Security Act of 1974 (ERISA).

If you have a good job and a good retirement plan, you could have a lot of money. You could lose a lot of money if your spouse is seeking part of your plan. In certain situations you may be able to offer your spouse some other asset instead of rights to part of your retirement plan. Filing a QDRO is a complex process that should be handled by attorneys.

After all of the paperwork is filed, a plan administrator will review the QDRO to ensure that it is in compliance with regulations. At this point, the plan administrator will determine each party's share in the fund. In determining each party's share, the plan administrator will consider whether or not the spouse who has the retirement plan was enrolled in that retirement plan or pension before the marriage took place.

If the plan began before the marriage took place, the duration of the marriage as well as the duration of the plan itself will be taken into consideration when determining what belongs to whom. Because this is an intricate process, several months can pass from the date a divorce is entered to the final distribution of the retirement plan.

QDROs can help you plan for your future and can be extremely helpful for a spouse that does not have a job or who does not make a lot of money. In some cases, you may have to give a part of your pension plan to your spouse. In other cases, you might receive money from a pension plan that your spouse has.

QDROs can help you claim your retirement plan and will give you and your spouse a fair portion of the fund.

Dividing The House

Figuring out who gets to keep major assets in divorce can be a struggle. Arguably your biggest asset is your home and property. So, who gets this in divorce? Consider a few different circumstances to figure this out.

The division of major assets such as your house will depend on if it is considered individual or communal property. For example, if you bought a home before you got married with your individual funds, the house would be considered your individual property. Likewise, if the home you live in was given to you alone as inheritance, the house is your individual property. If you and your spouse bought your home together over the course of your marriage, and both of your names are on the title deed and the mortgage, the house will be considered communal or marital property.

In most cases, marital property will be split 50/50. Since you both put money into the house, you are both entitled to the property. If only your name is on the title deed, but you bought the house over the course of your marriage and you and your spouse lived in the home as a marital residence, this gives your spouse some claim to the home.

This does not mean that your spouse is entitled to the money from selling the house. But, it does mean that you cannot force your spouse out of the house or sell the home without telling your spouse, so long as you are still legally married. Once you are divorced, you will be able to do with the house what you want. As you can see, your individual circumstances will determine who is entitled to keep the house in divorce.

In some cases, even if the house is marital property, you might be able to divide this asset in a way that allows you to get more money than your spouse.

Major changes are upon you if you are getting a divorce and selling your home. If you are selling your home for a fresh start, this process can't go fast enough. One thing to do before selling your home is get an appraisal on it.

An appraisal is an estimate made of your property's market value. An appraisal is done by an appraiser. The figure that the appraiser comes up with is based on sale prices for similar houses in your area. It is also based on the condition that your property is in. An appraiser will determine the market value of your property based on:

- Income approach: The income approach isn't generally used for residential properties, but it is still worthwhile to understand. The income approach works by determining the net income of the property and using this to estimate the property's value.
- Comparison approach: The comparison approach takes into consideration what properties similar to yours have sold for. Obviously, your house will differ in some ways from the houses and properties taken into account during the comparison. But, the appraiser takes these differences into consideration.
- Cost approach: This approach makes an estimation of the improvements that have been made on the property. This estimation is added to the value of the property to determine the full value.

The lender will hire an appraiser and use their estimations to decide on a loan that is appropriate. The lender does this so that they can have an unbiased estimation of the property's value. This happens before deciding to make a loan. You can have your house appraised by an appraiser that you hire, but a lender probably won't use your appraiser's estimates. This is because they will want to have their own appraisal done.

There aren't too many ways that you can prepare for an appraisal. The only thing that you can really do is make sure that if you're having maintenance done on your property, it is complete by the time the appraiser comes. Informing the appraiser of renovations and home improvements that you have made can help to increase the market value decided on. Providing assistance to the appraiser is also a good idea. Touring the property with them will give you the chance to explain the features of the property (both good and bad). It will also answer any questions that the appraiser might have.

Getting an appraisal on your home is a basic part of selling it. If you and your ex-spouse are still on good terms, you can work together. This will benefit both of you in the long run.

In this time of confusion, it might seem like too much to have to go through this difficult process AND sell the house. Here are some pros and cons of staying in your marital home.

Pros:

- Security: In the midst of all this change, it will be comforting to at least remain in the same house.
- Routine for the kids: You're not the only one who has to adjust to divorce. Maintaining a stable home life and routine for your kids is always a good idea. Staying in your house can help with that.
- Standard of living: You're accustomed to a certain standard of living, and you have a right to that standard even after divorce. Remaining in your house could help you maintain that standard.

Cons:

- What does your spouse think? Will your spouse let you keep the house? Or will they fight you tooth and nail for it? It might not be worth it to draw out yet another issue.
- Costs: After you get a divorce, you might not be able to afford to pay rent or make mortgage payments – at least not right away.
- Memories: Divorce means a fresh start. Getting that might be difficult if you live in a house filled with memories from your marriage.

If you decide that living in the marital residence is not the right choice for you, you have two other options. You can sell the home, or give the house title/mortgage to your ex. If your ex wants to continue living in the marital residence, they can buy you out. You'll get your share of the home equity and you can hand over the house title and mortgage to your ex. Or, the two of you can sell the house and split the profits.

It is important to have an understanding of your home equity whether you are getting a divorce or not. However, if you *are* getting a divorce, you probably realize that you and your spouse are going to have to split your assets. Yes, this includes splitting your home equity.

Splitting up assets can be a difficult process for you and your spouse. It is important to keep in mind that dividing home equity will depend on a lot of different variables. Each case is truly unique depending on what factors you brought to your marriage and buying your house.

Years ago, when you were a newlywed and you were buying your home, you may have been talked into not signing the house title by your lovely new spouse. For many people, this scenario is all too familiar. If this has happened to you, and you now face divorce, what happens next?

Even if only your spouse's name is on the deed, you have a legal right to occupy that home for as long as the two of you are married. The trouble occurs if you and your spouse decide to get a divorce. If your name is not on the deed, you do not have a legal right to the property.

However, this does not mean that all is lost. In many cases, equity is still split between both parties, even if your name is not on the deed. If you are about to get a divorce and you realize that your name is not on the house title, you should be proactive. If you lived in the house, you should file a Notice of Home Rights with the Land Registry. This will ensure that your spouse doesn't try to sell the house without letting you know. While you are still married, you have the right to know what is happening with the property, and it cannot be sold without your consent. Even if only your spouse's name is on the deed, you have a legal right to occupy that home for as long as the two of you are married.

Unfortunately, once you are divorced, if your name is not on the house title, you will not have a legal right to the house. However, you can fight for half of the home equity. Chances are that you will want a fresh start after your divorce, so even if you are unable to live in your old home, it might be a blessing in disguise, as it will help you close that chapter in your life and begin the next one.

Will The Court Intervene?

The easiest way to divide your assets and debt is by sitting down with your spouse and your lawyers and coming to a decision outside of court. This is because a court might impose a ruling that you or your spouse do not find satisfactory. If a judge orders for you to divide your assets in a certain way, you must do it.

It is oftentimes easier to try to sort things out without involving a judge. In some cases, this can make both parties happier. If you and your spouse are on good terms and you are both willing to make sacrifices in order to have your debt and asset division settled outside of court, you should take advantage of this option. However, if you and your spouse are not on good terms, and you think that one or both of you will fight over property and debt, a judge will have to intervene and divide your assets and debt for you.

If you and your spouse do take your case to court, you need to be prepared to fight for your assets. In order to do this, you should present proof of your separate property as well as reasons why you deserve at least half if not more of your marital property.

For your separate property, you should present the judge with evidence of when you purchased that property and show that you alone purchased it. If you were married in 2000 and you purchased a house in 1997, show the judge that the house is indeed separate property due to the date of purchase. You will then have to determine if your spouse has added any value to the equity in the property and the current value of the property. These are just some of the basics to consider.

If you feel that you deserve at least half or more of your marital property, but you believe that your spouse should take on more than half of your marital debt, you need to prove why this is the case to a judge. Showing a judge documents such as your bank statements, other proof of your financial situation, and your work history can help if you believe that your spouse is in a better position to take on the debt. Keep in mind that taking your case to court could result in a decision that you are unhappy with. For this reason, it is important to build a strong case to defend your reasoning and prove to a judge why you deserve certain assets.

CHAPTER 6:

Child Custody Issues

I've outlined many points thus far that are important in divorce, but this chapter will deal with what many people consider the most important aspect of divorce - child custody. If you and your spouse have children together, you probably have a million questions running through your mind. These are just a few of the questions you're probably asking, and questions that I will answer in this chapter:

- What are my custody options?
- Will I receive child custody?
- What if my spouse is abusive – can I ensure that they don't get custody?
- Will I have to pay child support? If so, how much?
- Will I receive visitation rights?

It is important to understand that each divorce is different. Your case will be unique and there is no one answer to these questions. However, I can help you learn about your options and the potential outcomes that you face.

The first thing that you should consider when deciding who will have custody of your child is if you and your spouse can work this issue out on your own, or if you need a judge to decide for you. If you and your spouse are fairly amicable and are on the same page concerning custody, there is no need to begin a custody battle.

Custody battles can be stressful and expensive. However, if you and your spouse cannot settle custody issues outside of court, presenting your case and having a judge decide questions of custody might be your best option. If you and your spouse take your custody battle to court, a judge will be in control of your custody situation. A judge will review the facts of your case and determine who should receive what type of custody with your child's best interest in mind.

Sometimes, in order to protect your child's interests, a judge will appoint a guardian ad litem for your child. When a custody battle goes to court, both spouses generally hire attorneys to represent their interests. But the question is: who will represent your child's interests in an unbiased and professional manner? If both parents believe that they should receive sole or primary custody of the child, how will the court determine what the child's best interests actually are?

This is where a guardian ad litem comes in. A guardian ad litem can be appointed to a case by a judge, or one can be requested by an attorney or parent. Fees are typically charged by the hour and paid for by the parents of the child. Whether a guardian ad litem is appointed or not, a judge will determine the most stable and healthy environment for your child based on the facts presented in court. A court can order sole custody to one parent, primary custody to either parent, or shared physical custody of the minor child.

The two major types of custody are the ones I've mentioned above – legal and physical custody. Sometimes people get these types of custody mixed up, so I would like to clarify which is which here. Legal custody refers to a parent's ability to be involved in making decisions regarding their child. If you have legal custody over your child, you can be involved in making medical, educational, religious and other decisions.

However, this type of custody has nothing to do with whom your child lives with. Just because you have legal custody of your child does not mean that they will automatically reside with you. The type of custody that refers to where your child lives is physical custody. If you receive physical custody, your child will primarily live with you. In some cases, you might be denied physical custody but given legal custody. This will depend on your personal situation.

Sole custody is full legal and physical custody given to one parent in the event that the other parent is deemed unfit or unable to raise a child by the court. In most cases, such a finding is determined by a history of instability in character or an inability to provide for the child's needs by one spouse proven to the court by the other spouse.

Some examples of ways that a parent can lose custody of their child are issues with alcohol or drugs, and violent tendencies. Particularly if a parent has abused their child, whether sexually, emotionally, or physically, that parent can be at serious risk for losing custody of the child. Furthermore, if one parent endangers the life or well-being of their child through erratic behavior or poor decision-making, custody can be revoked.

Another way that a parent can lose custody is if they abandon or neglect their child. In some cases, sole custody is necessary in order to protect a child from one unstable parent. However, in recent years, fewer and fewer custody battles have ended in sole custody rulings. This is because the court recognizes how important it is for a child to have both parents in their life, even if these parents are divorced.

When possible, judges will award primary physical custody to one parent with visitation to another, so long as both parents are fit to raise their child. This ensures that the child can maintain a relationship with each parent. Sole custody could refer to sole physical custody, sole legal custody, or both.

As a parent, you have certain rights and responsibilities toward your child. Even if you are going through a divorce, these rights will be protected unless you are deemed an unfit parent by the court (in which case you could lose legal or physical custody of your child, or both). Despite the fact that many mothers get primary physical custody of their child, this does not change the fact that mothers and fathers both have the same rights and responsibilities. As a parent, you have the following obligations toward your children:

- You must provide medical treatment for your child.
- You must provide schooling for your child.
- You must support your child financially.
- You must provide necessities such as shelter, food, and clothing.
- You must love, nurture, and encourage your child.
- You must protect your child from neglect or harm.

- You must improve the relationship of your child with their other parent.

If a court determines that you have violated any of these obligations, you could lose your rights as a parent. These rights include:

- Participating in parenting.
- Being involved in your child's life.
- Deciding where your child lives.
- Viewing your child's medical records.
- Having custody of your child.
- Viewing your child's school records.
- Making decisions concerning religion, schooling, and the medical treatment of your child.

In some divorces, parental rights can be modified. Joint physical and shared legal custody is another option that you have when dividing custody between you and your spouse. This type of custody will allow you and your spouse to make joint decisions regarding your child's religion, health, education, and even what activities they are involved in. This means that you and your spouse will share the responsibility of raising your child, even though you are no longer married.

If you have shared physical custody as well as joint legal custody, your child will live with both of you at different times. For example, a child might live with one parent during weekdays and another on weekends. Another example is that the child lives with each parent for a full week and rotates each week. If one spouse relocates, physical custody can be split up differently, for example, one parent can exercise physical custody during the school year and the other parent will get physical custody during summer months.

A major benefit of shared physical custody is that your child will be able to maintain their relationship with both parents. This can ease a child's transition into life after divorce and can help the child understand that despite the divorce, they are still loved by both parents.

Just as with sole custody, joint custody can differ when factoring in legal and physical custody. If parents have full joint custody, they share both physical and legal custody. However, sometimes courts will appoint joint legal custody but not joint physical custody.

Full joint custody (joint legal custody and joint physical custody) is the most popular legal custody arrangement by Connecticut courts, however this type of custody can have serious consequences if one parent is not involved in their child's life or if both parents cannot communicate well and agree on decisions involving the child. If you and your spouse get along well and you recognize the importance of a child having both parents in their life, joint legal custody might be the right option for you. However, if one spouse in a divorce case is abusive and is unfit to have custody of their child, the court will most likely award sole legal custody to the more stable parent.

The court always takes a position regarding the children as to what is in their best interest. There is a factor test that the court or a guardian ad litem considers when looking at the best interest of the children for custody purposes.

Visitation

Under Connecticut law, persons with significant ties to children have visitation rights. Recently, the Connecticut Supreme Court ruled that grandparents and others must demonstrate that they have a "parent-like" relationship with the child if they want visitation rights. They must prove that the child will suffer harm if visitation is denied. This is a heavy burden of proof. It will have a significant impact on the ability of third-parties to obtain visitation orders.

As a divorced parent, you might have primary custody of your children. If this is the case, you will have the opportunity to be very involved in your child's life. You will be able to see them on a regular basis. You will also have the primary responsibility of taking care of your child.

On the other hand, you might be the non-custodial parent and only have visitation rights. This can make maintaining a relationship with your child and staying involved in their life difficult. If you have visitation rights, it is important to understand what type of visitation you have. This will help you plan your visits accordingly.

There are three major types of visitation. The first is unsupervised visitation. This is the type of visitation that is most commonly awarded in divorce cases. If you received unsupervised visitation rights from a court, it means that you will be able to take your children to your new home or on special outings without the intervention of the court.

Keep in mind that just because these visitations are not supervised does not mean that they can occur at any time. You still have to stick to a regular visitation schedule. In some situations, certain restrictions can be placed on unsupervised visitations. For example, if you have a very young child who is still breastfeeding, you might be asked to conduct your visits at their primary house until the child is more self-sufficient.

Another type of visitation is supervised visitation. If you can only conduct supervised visitations, it means that another adult has to be present during your visits with your children. In some cases, you will be able to appoint the supervisor of these visits. For example, you could choose your child's grandparent or another family member to act as a supervisor.

In other cases, this supervision is more strict. The court will appoint a social worker or some other designee to be present during your visits. In more relaxed cases, you can still meet with your child in your own home or out on the town. In other cases, the court will appoint a location for you to conduct your visitations. Supervised visitation can be awkward, but try to make your child as comfortable with the situation as possible.

One fairly new type of visitation is virtual visitation. Virtual visitation comes in the form of communicating through email, social media, text messaging, or Skyping. This type of visitation is less common than supervised or unsupervised visitation.

Parenting Education Programs

The state of Connecticut requires all parents involved in divorce to attend a parenting program. This request is court ordered, and if you fail to attend the parenting program, legal action can be taken against you.

Parenting Education Programs (PEP) are classes that seek to help parents understand and properly address issues that a child experiences when their parents get divorced. A PEP will show parents how to help their child deal with the divorce in a healthy way, ultimately improving the child's relationship with both parents.

Parents involved in other litigation can also be asked to attend a parenting program. If you face any of the following, the court can ask you to enroll in a PEP:

- Annulment.
- Dissolution.
- Custody case.
- Visitation case.
- Legal separation.

All parents with children who are under the age of eighteen are court mandated to participate in a PEP. You must be enrolled in a parenting program within 60 days after your divorce is filed with the court.

To register for a parenting education program, you have to fill out the Parenting Education Program Order, Certificate, and Results Form. You can obtain this form at a judicial district clerk's office, the judicial branch's website, or a court service center. Some lawyers or the program itself might also provide this form.

Once you fill out this form, you should contact the program director to ask about additional registration information, when and where the class takes place, and the program's fees. You should bring a parenting education certification form with you to your classes and when you complete the program, this should be signed. This will show a court that you adequately completed the program.

CHAPTER 7:

Support Issues

When couples decide to get divorced, they will oftentimes go before a judge in a short hearing so that they can get important issues resolved temporarily. This is known as temporary orders. The purpose of temporary orders is to keep your family as close to its status quo as possible during the divorce process. This is achieved by setting up temporary spousal support, child support, or child custody.

If you want to request temporary orders, you should think about what you are entitled to in your divorce. Then, you will have to present your case to a judge. In most cases, you will only have a few minutes to discuss the temporary orders with a judge, so make sure that you can present a brief and concise case.

If you request temporary orders during your divorce case, your request will be put on the court calendar and a hearing will quickly be scheduled for you. In most cases, a hearing will be scheduled within 2-3 weeks of filing the necessary motions. Temporary orders are valid until another hearing is held to change them or until both spouses come to a more permanent agreement in their divorce.

Temporary orders can be replaced by longstanding orders of child support and spousal support. Most couples that take their divorce cases to court do so because they cannot come to a decision on who should pay support and what type of support to pay. If you and your spouse have children together, you will probably continue communicating with one another even after your divorce is finalized. At the very least, you will still be connected financially, because you will both be responsible for supporting your children. In addition, some spouses have to pay spousal support, also known as alimony, after divorce.

There are many different types of child support and alimony, and which type, if any, is awarded to your case will depend on many factors that contributed to your marriage and the breakdown of the marriage.

Child Support

If you are going through a divorce, and you and your spouse have children together, one major decision that you have to make is how parental access will be determined. While child custody cases have a nasty reputation, not all are mean spirited and drawn out. As stated in the previous section, you have several options when determining child custody. Regardless of what you want, you should be thinking about what is in the best interest of your child. In some cases, depending on the setup of parental access, this will mean that one parent pays child support to the other.

You've probably seen movies where child support is paid after a divorce, or you might know someone who pays child support - but what exactly is it, and how is it determined? If you have been asked by your spouse or a judge to pay child support, you need to know exactly what is expected of you.

Child support is usually a fixed amount of money that you pay in order to care for and support your child after divorce. Just as with spousal support, child support is temporary and will last until the child turns 18 or graduates from high school, whichever is later. Child support is awarded to the custodial parent.

Child support is based specifically on financials of the parties. It is a calculation that takes into account the parties' incomes, payment of certain additional fees such as health insurance and union dues, and the number of children from the marriage.

Divorce oftentimes represents a big change for children. Many children feel like their lives have been uprooted when they learn that their parents are getting a divorce. Child support is meant to help children through this difficult time by allowing them to maintain their standard of living from before the divorce. This helps them adjust to their new lifestyle and allows aspects of their lives to remain the same.

Because child support is determined by concrete financial information, it is one of the easiest calculations to make in a divorce.

In Connecticut, child support is mandatory by statute and is dependent on a calculation system. The numbers do not have much flexibility. The party that will pay child support is the non-custodial parent. The parent that has primary custody of the child will not be asked to pay child support because they will be living with and providing for the child on a regular basis.

If you have to take your case to court, the judge will generally ask you to provide a financial statement. This will help the judge presiding over your case understand your financial situation. Your spouse will be asked to provide the same information, giving the judge a complete picture of the financial situation involved in the case.

When determining who pays child support, and how much is paid, the court may take a few other factors into consideration. Most importantly, the needs of your child will be considered. How much money is required to adequately support your child will determine how much money is to be paid. But how is this figure determined?

As I briefly touched on before, an evaluation of you and your spouse's income will be done to determine your financial situation. Child support is calculated based on both parents' gross income. Deductibles can be made from both the mother and the father's income in order to determine what they can realistically afford to pay in terms of child support. Some deductibles that might be taken into account are the value of a federal dependency exemption (if applicable), the sum of income tax that is actually paid, and alimony or child support that are being paid from a separate divorce.

Once these factors are taken into consideration, the gross income is adjusted to take variations into account. This chart will help determine how much child support is needed by evaluating the income category that you are in and how much money a child typically needs within this category.

Child support is a court order and once it is put into place, you will be legally bound to make these payments. If you are asked to make child support payments, you will be in contact with the child support division of the court. In order to check up on you, regular compliance reviews can be filed with the child support division. Support Enforcement Services can monitor your child support payments, if necessary. If you have a history of making late payments, you will probably receive a reminder from this division before your child support payments are due.

If you fail to make your child support payments, the child support division of the court can file a contempt proceeding. Failing to pay your child support payments can be very serious. In some cases, you could face incarceration. This can happen if a court determines that you intentionally violated a court order for child support. The court can imprison you for this and will set an amount that you must pay in order to be released from incarceration. In most cases, the possibility of incarceration alone will make people pay their child support. However, this is not always the case.

If the child support division feels that you are in contempt of the court and you are knowingly refusing to make your child support payments, a hearing will be scheduled. During this hearing, the child support division will show cause as to how you are in contempt of the court. It will have to be proven that you received notice of your child support payments, that you have the ability to pay, and that you refused to do so during this hearing.

At this hearing, you have the right to show cause as to why you are not in contempt of the court. If you are called in for such a hearing, you should consider contacting an attorney to represent you in court, as losing this case could mean jail time.

As you can see, you will face serious consequences if you disregard court ordered child support and refuse to pay it. The best thing that you can do is to pay the support in order to avoid problems. You do not want to risk serving jail time for failure to pay child support. If the child support division contacts you about problems with your child support payments, make sure that you pay the child support immediately.

Remember - child support is based on your income. So if you are not paying your child support because you have lost your job or your income decreased, you need to immediately notify the court. The court can make a modification to your child support plan if it knows what is going on. However, if you do not update the court with your financial standings, you can be charged with refusal to pay child support.

Ideally, the court will be able to determine child support payments that you can afford. However, this is not always the case. Certain expenses may be unpredictable or they may not be included in the initial determination of your finances. You can talk to your attorney about what you can and cannot afford.

In most divorce cases, the non-custodial parent will have to pay child support until their child is an adult. A child is considered an adult when they graduate from high school or when they turn 18, but at no time later than when the child turns 19. Events such as remarriage or moving out-of-state are not excuses to stop paying child support.

Likewise, if your child moves out-of-state, this does not mean that you can stop paying child support. If your child moves out-of-state, the new state that they live in will begin enforcing your child support order.

Federal law requires child support enforcement agencies in different states to help one another collect child support. This is because collecting child support when the non-custodial parent and the child live in different states is a more difficult process. It can take more time for the payments to be received and distributed, so these agencies help each other collect the support and make the process as easy as possible.

If your child moves and you are unsure as to how to make your child support payments, you can contact the child support enforcement division. This division of the court will help any parent or guardian who has a child under the age of eighteen and will do their best to make sure that the child support reaches the child in a timely manner.

If, on the other hand, you are a parent seeking child support from your ex-spouse who now lives in another state, you have two ways that you can go about collecting it. The first way is to ask the court to set a child support order if your ex-spouse hasn't been making payments since they moved. The second option is to have a legal document sent to the state where your ex-spouse lives. This petition will alert your ex-spouse to the fact that they need to continue paying the child support.

While moving out of state is not a valid excuse to stop paying child support, there are some other cases where you can stop making payments before your child is an adult. It is important to keep in mind that these situations in which you would stop having to pay child support are relatively rare.

One way that you will be relieved of your child support duties is if your child becomes an emancipated minor. If your child is emancipated, this means that they are legally separated from both you and their other parent, in which case you will no longer be expected to provide for this child.

Another event that could terminate your responsibility to pay child support is if your child gets married before the age of eighteen. At this point, it will be the responsibility of your child's spouse to take care of them.

One other way that your obligation to pay child support can end is if your child enters the armed services and is placed on active duty. In addition, if there is a termination of a party's parental rights, this will stop child support.

Obviously, in any of these situations, you can still make the choice to help support your child. However, you will not be legally bound to do so. Likewise, in the case that you want to continue supporting your child after they are legally considered an adult, this is possible. It will be up to you to continue making child support payments or to terminate them after your child turns eighteen. Many parents choose to help their children pay for college or rent their first apartment. If this is something that you want to do, you could continue paying child support while your child is in their twenties.

Spousal Support

When you get married, you and your spouse promise to support each other for the rest of your lives. This promise forces married couples to make certain decisions for their families. For example, you might choose to stay at home to raise your children, knowing that your spouse will support you. Or, you might get a particular job so that you can provide for your spouse. These decisions will impact you and your spouse, even after you are divorced. Some of these decisions could lead to the need for spousal support in your divorce.

First off, it is important to understand under what circumstances spousal support, also known as "alimony", will be paid. If, over the course of your marriage, you and your spouse both worked, had similar incomes, and had some independent finances, alimony may not be awarded to your case. This is because there won't be a need for alimony in this situation.

The purpose of alimony is to keep both parties at a comparable level financially to where they were during their marriage. For example, spousal support can be awarded in a divorce case if you had a lengthy marriage in which one spouse worked while the other stayed at home. The stay-at-home spouse probably has outdated job skills or no job skills at all, no individual pension, and limited ways of finding a job. The stay-at-home spouse in the relationship might receive alimony in a divorce to help them pay bills while they find a job. Here is the definition of alimony as provided by the Connecticut General Assembly:

Sec. 46b-82. (Formerly Sec. 46-52). Alimony. (a) At the time of entering the decree, the Superior Court may order either of the parties to pay alimony to the other, in addition to or in lieu of an award pursuant to section 46b-81. The order may direct that security be given therefore on such terms as the court may deem desirable, including an order pursuant to subsection (b) of this section or an order to either party to contract with a third party for periodic payments or payments contingent on a life to the other party. The court may order that a party obtain life insurance as such security unless such party proves, by a preponderance of the evidence, that such insurance is not available to such party, such party is unable to pay the cost of such insurance or such party is uninsurable. In determining whether alimony shall be awarded, and the duration and amount of the award, the court shall consider the evidence presented by each party and shall consider the length of the marriage, the causes for the annulment, dissolution of the marriage or legal separation, the age, health, station, occupation, amount and sources of income, earning capacity, vocational skills, education, employability, estate and needs of each of the parties and the award, if any, which the court may make pursuant to section 46b-81, and, in the case of a parent to whom the custody of minor children has been awarded, the desirability and feasibility of such parent's securing employment.

(b) If the court, following a trial or hearing on the merits, enters an order pursuant to subsection (a) of this section, or section 46b-86, and such order by its terms will terminate only upon the death of either party or the remarriage of the alimony recipient, the court shall articulate with specificity the basis for such order.

(c) Any postjudgment procedure afforded by chapter 906 shall be available to secure the present and future financial interests of a party in connection with a final order for the periodic payment of alimony.

There are different types of spousal support that will be awarded depending on your personal situation. Some types of alimony only last for a few months or years. Others can last for much longer.

One type of spousal support is temporary spousal support, also referred to as pendente lite. In order to receive this type of spousal support, you will have to file temporary orders during the process of your divorce. This type of alimony allows both spouses to maintain their lifestyles while they are going through this difficult process. This is achieved by having the spouse that makes more money pay support to the spouse that doesn't. Temporary spousal support will occur in a situation like the one I listed above, where one spouse makes much more money than the other. Temporary spousal support is especially common in situations where only one spouse in the relationship has a job.

Temporary spousal support is exactly what it sounds like – temporary. When your divorce is finalized, these payments will no longer be made. This is because the spouse that is not currently working or who has a low income is expected to begin working or get a job that can support them when the divorce is over.

Another form of alimony is called periodic alimony. If you had temporary spousal support during your divorce, you will probably be awarded periodic alimony when the divorce is finalized. This type of spousal support is paid to the spouse with the lower earnings during the marriage. The divorce will clearly change this spouse's income and lifestyle. This spouse will receive spousal support for a certain period of time and in a certain amount.

Periodic alimony typically ends after a certain amount of years. Alimony also can terminate upon the receiving spouses' remarriage, and in some circumstances, cohabitation. Cohabitation means that you or your ex are in a new relationship and now live with the new significant other.

Another type of alimony is rehabilitative alimony. This spousal support is paid to the spouse that didn't work during the marriage. Because of divorce, this spouse will have to get a job in order to support themselves. While this spouse gets job training, job experience, or furthers their education, they will receive spousal support.

This type of alimony is meant to help a spouse that has no job experience or skills. It helps them until they become self-sufficient. Also, this type of spousal support is usually set for a fixed period of time. This happens because it is only meant as a temporary fix to help one spouse become self-sufficient.

Then there is reimbursement alimony. This is meant to reimburse one spouse for expenses paid for the other spouse. This includes payment for a college degree or medical school. If you spent money to help build your spouse's career and are no longer receiving the benefits of their career because of your divorce, you could get reimbursement alimony.

One other type of spousal support is called permanent alimony. While the previous types of spousal support mentioned are meant to be temporary, this type of support, as the name suggests, is permanent. Permanent alimony can only be terminated by one of two events. The first is if one of the parties involved in the agreement dies. The other is if the party that receives the spousal support remarries. Sometimes cohabitation could end such alimony award.

Despite the fact that permanent alimony is rarely terminated, it can be adjusted based on the financial situation of both the payer and the recipient. For example, if the payer gets a promotion, the recipient can petition for larger payments. The logic here would be that the person paying the alimony would be in a position to pay more without having it affect their financial standings.

On the other hand, if the person paying the alimony loses their job, or if they take a pay cut, a petition can be made to have the alimony amount decreased. In this situation, the person paying the alimony would argue that they are no longer in a position to pay the same amount as in the past without having it dramatically impact their finances.

Permanent alimony, also known as lifetime alimony, is unlikely to be awarded in many cases. The length of the marriage and the disproportionate amount of income and assets are some of the main considerations when the court decides upon an award of lifetime alimony. Many times, even if lifetime alimony is awarded, the court allows for re-evaluation upon the paying party's retirement.

Alimony is typically modifiable. This means that upon a substantial change of circumstances, the award of alimony, amount, and terms could be modified with good cause. You should consult with your attorney to make sure specific provisions are in your divorce agreement to specify if alimony is modifiable.

CHAPTER 8:

Alternatives To Litigation

If you've definitely decided that you want to get a divorce, there are a few ways that you can go through the divorce process. Two major ways to deal with your divorce are through bringing your case to court or settling the divorce outside of court. Even if you're ready for a divorce, you might not be mentally or financially prepared for a hostile battle in court. If this is the case, it is important to keep in mind that there are alternatives to divorce battles in court.

Before discussing alternatives to litigation, I want to touch on alternatives to divorce. In some situations, an annulment is a better option for a couple than a divorce. Consider if this is the right choice for your situation.

Annulment

Divorce and annulment have similarities, however, they are also two different procedures that can mean slightly different things. Both are court proceedings that dissolve a marriage, however, a divorce implies that the marriage has simply ended, while an annulment treats the marriage like it never happened. Because divorce can carry a negative stigma, some people prefer to have their marriages annulled. If this is the case, a civil annulment is applied for.

However, some people want to get an annulment because it makes it easier to remarry within the church if the marriage is not recognized. If this is the case, you should get a religious annulment. If you want to get a civil annulment, there are several grounds that you can file for an annulment on. These vary slightly by state, so you should hire a divorce attorney to help you understand the exact laws and procedures in your state. However, getting an annulment will generally require at least one of the following reasons.

The first reason to get a civil annulment is fraud or misrepresentation. If your spouse knowingly lied to you about something like their ability to have children, a previous or existing marriage, or reaching the age of consent, these are grounds for an annulment. Another reason to get an annulment is the ability or refusal to consummate the marriage. If your marriage is never consummated, for whatever reason, you will have grounds for an annulment.

Concealment is another grounds for an annulment. If your spouse conceals an addiction to drugs or alcohol, children from another relationship, a sexually transmitted disease, a felony conviction, or impotency, you might be able to get an annulment. The final grounds for an annulment is a misunderstanding, such as if one spouse wants to have children and the other does not. This is the most open-ended of the reasons for an annulment, so you might want to talk to a lawyer about your specific circumstances and the likelihood of making a case for an annulment.

The other type of annulment is religious annulment. This occurs within the Roman Catholic Church. If a couple gets a civil annulment, they will be eligible to obtain a religious annulment as well. This will make it easier for one or both people to remarry within the Catholic Church or any other place. However, just because you get a civil annulment does not mean that you will automatically get a religious one. There are different grounds for religious annulment than a civil one.

Generally, annulments take place after a short period of time. Usually, married couples get an annulment within the first few weeks or months after the marriage took place. This means that there are not many assets to divide among them. Annulments that occur when the marriage is long-term can be more difficult, as there will be assets to divide.

"There must be a deception in respect to some fact whose existence or nonexistence may affect in some certain way the very essence of the marriage relation, resulting in a lawful marriage which practically operates as a fraud upon the deceived spouse; and the existence or nonexistence of the fact thus concealed or misrepresented must operate, as between parties to the marriage, to prevent some essential purpose of marriage and work a practical destruction of that relation". Gould v. Gould, 78 Conn. 242, 261 (1905).

"In Connecticut, by statute . . . fraudulent contract is a ground for divorce. This ground probably embraces some situations which, at least in jurisdictions not having such a ground of divorce, could also support an action for annulment". Perlstein v. Perlstein, 152 Conn. 152, 161, 204 A.2d 909 (1964).

"All the grounds of divorce specified, except fraudulent contract, are of such a nature that they can come into existence only after the marriage. While fraudulent conduct of a certain kind will render a marriage voidable, such fraud differs from that which vitiates ordinary contracts in that the party defrauded may not at his own election avoid the marriage, but it is held to be voidable only by a decree of the court". Davis v. Davis, 119 Conn. 194, 196, 175 A. 574 (1934).

If this applies to you, you may qualify for an annulment and may want to pursue an annulment. Remember, in order to receive an annulment you must be able to prove to the court there was some type of fraud, mistake, or misconception.

Mediation

If you want to get a divorce, but you don't want to go through litigation, mediation is an option. Mediation is a widely accepted strategy for dealing with divorce. It will allow you and your spouse to settle your differences outside of court, saving you and your children a lot of trauma and potentially saving you money on lengthy court appearances. If you are in the process of getting a divorce and you and your spouse are fairly amicable, mediation might be the right option for you.

Mediation allows you and your spouse to sit down together and work through the divorce process. This is achieved with the help of a neutral mediator whose job is to help you work out your issues. Before you decide to use mediation as a divorce strategy, you should speak with your spouse about this option.

Only you and your spouse would know best if you can handle an amicable process by compromising and talking through your issues with a mediator. If you and your spouse are dealing with a messy divorce and have a difficult time communicating, mediation might not be the right choice for you. Some couples begin the mediation process but are unable to finish it due to their differences of opinion. If issues are left unresolved after mediation or if mediation is cut short, you and your spouse must then enter your divorce in court anyway. Make sure that mediation is right for you because you could waste time and money if mediation does not work.

If you do determine that you and your spouse can handle mediation, you should hire a mediator. Many groups in Connecticut offer mediation services. The mediator is a neutral party during these sessions, which means that they will not take sides in your case. Even if one party is clearly wrong in some aspect, the mediator will not take sides. The mediator will only point out issues that need to be resolved and aspects of the divorce process that each spouse should be aware of so that both parties can be satisfied with the divorce. The mediator will help both spouses negotiate their issues.

Mediators are trained to help people resolve conflicts that may arise over divorce issues such as dividing assets and debt, child custody, child support, alimony, and more. The goal of mediation is not necessarily a settlement. Mediators only want to ensure that an agreement is reached that pleases both you and your spouse.

If you are nervous about mediation, you may have a lawyer present so that you can feel confident in the decisions you are making. You can always refer to a professional attorney with your questions. Please remember that a mediator cannot provide the parties with legal advice and you may want your own attorney to advise you through the mediation process.

Many people choose mediation in their divorces because it has several benefits. One benefit is that mediation allows spouses to maintain some form of a relationship throughout their divorce and even after. Instead of constantly fighting and threatening one another, mediation allows spouses to sit down together and communicate about what they want from the divorce. Maintaining a friendly relationship is especially important if you and your spouse have children together. Making important decisions about your children is easier when you and your ex are on good terms. You will have a greater sense of control in the divorce process.

Another benefit of mediation is that it is oftentimes easier on your children than traditional litigation. Divorce can be a traumatic experience for children, mostly due to the fact that it disrupts their routines. If you and your spouse make the divorce process as quick and easy as possible, and show your children that you are still invested in maintaining a relationship, the divorce will be easier for your children.

Lastly, mediation is a good choice because it is effective. Couples that take advantage of mediation are more likely to be satisfied with the divorce process and the results of the divorce because they feel like they are directly involved in the decisions made in divorce. Mediation allows spouses to remain in control at a time when they might feel overwhelmed or powerless.

Arbitration

When searching for an alternative to litigation in a divorce case, you might be considering mediation or arbitration. While these are similar strategies that can help you resolve issues with your spouse outside of court, they are different in some important ways.

Keep in mind that mediation does not impose any decision onto a couple. A mediator is only present to help the couple resolve their issues in a healthy, fair way. Arbitration, on the other hand, can impose a settlement on a couple. Understanding arbitration as well as mediation can help you make the right decision for your situation.

If you and your spouse decide to see an arbitrator to help you with your divorce, you must understand that the arbitrator can make decisions concerning your case. Before you go to an arbitrator, you must sign a document stating that you understand that you can't overturn the arbitrator's decision, regardless of your personal feelings about the decision. Once this document is signed, the arbitrator will listen to each spouse's case, and then render a ruling.

Many couples decide to use arbitration because it is usually much cheaper and quicker than taking the case to court. Instead of a judge deciding if one spouse wronged the other, an arbitrator does this. The arbitrator will decide how to compensate one spouse for the wrongdoing of the other.

But, keep in mind that you cannot appeal the decision of the arbitrator. Once an arbitrator reaches a decision, it will stand. Only under extremely limited circumstances will an arbitrator's decision get overturned.

If you are looking for a faster and cheaper way to settle differences that you and your spouse have in order to get on with your divorce, arbitration might be a good action for you to take. Keep in mind that that arbitrator can make a binding settlement that will be extremely difficult for you to fight if you are unhappy with it.

If you feel that you can present a clear, solid case to an arbitrator, you might save time and money by approaching an arbitrator rather than trying to get a court hearing with a judge. However, if you only want someone who will listen to the problems that you and your spouse face, and help you resolve them in a healthy, unbiased manner, then you should look for a mediator.

Discuss these options with your spouse and try to come to a conclusion together if possible. If you and your spouse are unsure how to handle your situation, discuss your options with a lawyer. This might help you to make the most informed decision.

Collaborative Divorce

Another alternative to divorce that is similar to mediation is collaborative divorce. Like many other alternatives to divorce, this is an option that can be pursued outside of court, which makes it attractive to many couples hoping to skip the drawn out court battles. Collaborative divorce is a form of conflict resolution in which couples take ownership of themselves, as opposed to having a judge intervene in their case.

Collaborative divorce attempts to give both parties involved in divorce the means to work out their issues and come to a mutual agreement. However, unlike in mediation, there is no neutral third party guiding the discussions and meetings. Instead, both parties meet with their lawyers and these parties work issues out amongst themselves.

In order to come to an agreement, both parties use informal methods to establish their arguments rather than formally bringing them to court. For example, if you feel that you deserve alimony, you can provide your spouse with your financial records directly as proof of why you need support, instead of showing this to a judge who will decide what to do. In order to help each spouse make a case, sometimes professionals like financial planners, counselors, and accountants can be called in. While this is not necessary, it can help you build a case in some situations.

A lot of couples turn to collaborative divorce because it can reduce stress as well as the costs spent on divorce. Because you aren't going to court, you don't have to worry about filing fees and the outcome of your divorce is in your hands instead of a judge's. In a time when you might feel helpless, gaining control of the outcome of your divorce can make all of the difference for your mental health.

Because you will have a lawyer with you, you can also have the peace of mind that you are making the right decision from a legal standpoint. The legal counsel involved in collaborative divorce is just as invested in protecting you as you are, so you can trust their advice. In addition, collaborative divorce can be much quicker than bringing your case to court, as you won't have to wait for court dates to be scheduled.

CHAPTER 9:

Expedited Divorce

Connecticut has recently implemented expedited divorce (also called non-adversarial divorce) in the state. This is a faster divorce process than traditional divorce. See if you qualify or if this is something that you are interested in by learning more here.

The new law in Connecticut allows for expedited divorce. This type of divorce allows a judge to speed up the process. In regular divorce cases, a hearing must take place before the divorce can properly be finalized. But, the non-adversarial divorce allows a judge to enter a decree without this hearing. This can speed up the process significantly. Couples who get an expedited divorce can finish the process in as few as 35 days. Compared to the months or even years that couples currently spend on divorce, the expedited process can make a huge difference.

In addition, couples can ask a judge to waive the waiting period involved in divorce. Traditionally, divorce proceedings could not begin until couples filed a motion which started a waiting period. This waiting period lasts for 90 days. The waiting period was designed to give couples a cooling off period before going ahead with a divorce. Divorce is a serious decision, and the courts wanted to make sure that couples who divorce have thought this through. But, in expedited divorce, the waiting period can be waived.

Another benefit of expedited divorce is that couples don't have to go to court to complete their divorce. Instead, a judge can grant divorce through paperwork alone.

In Connecticut, not all couples can apply for expedited divorce. Only couples that meet certain requirements will have the opportunity to file a non-adversarial divorce. The first requirement is that the couple's marriage lasted eight years or less. Next, at least one of the spouses in the marriage must be a resident of the state of Connecticut.

In addition, the couple must have no real estate. The total value of all property owned by either party has to be less than $35,000.

Also, neither spouse can have a company sponsored benefit pension plan. In addition, keep in mind that the couple cannot have any children in order to qualify. This also means that the couple cannot be pregnant when trying to file for an expedited divorce. In addition, neither spouse should have or apply for Medicaid benefits. Also, there should not be protective orders or restraining orders between the spouses. Finally, neither spouse can be in the middle of bankruptcy or another divorce.

You and your spouse might wonder if expedited divorce is right for your situation. There are a few factors to consider before you make this decision. First, make sure that you meet the qualifications for expedited divorce. If you don't qualify, you won't have any reason to consider this option. But, if you do qualify, you might take this option seriously. This could be a good option if you want to get your divorce over with as quickly as possible. Also, if you go through the expedited process, you won't have to go to court. This means that you won't have to take time off of work to go to the courthouse. Emotionally, finalizing your divorce quickly can also have benefits. It means that you can move on from your divorce as quickly as possible.

If you and your spouse determine that non-adversarial divorce is right for you, you need to file a non-adversarial divorce petition. You must completely fill out the following forms in order to apply.

- Form JD-FM-242. This is the joint petition form for non-adversarial divorce/the dissolution of marriage.
- Form JD-FM-6. This is a financial affidavit. Each spouse has to fill out a copy, meaning you have to fill out two copies. There are now two kinds of financial affidavit – one for those that make under $75,000 per year, and one for those who make over $75,000 per year. You should fill out the version of the form that applies to your situation.
- Form JD-FM-158. This is the notice of automatic court orders.

- Form JD-CL-12. This is an appearance form. Again, you have to fill out two copies of the form - one for each spouse.
- Form JD-FM-243. This form is the agreement form for non-adversarial divorce. In some cases, this form does not apply.
- Form JD-FM-175. This is the certificate of public assistance. It is also optional. It might not apply if your family has not received public assistance.

Make sure that you completely fill them out before sending them in. If there is information missing from the forms, they will be sent back to you. This will make the process of getting divorced longer. If you need help filling out these forms, contact a divorce lawyer.

CHAPTER 10:

Moving On After Divorce

If you've just finalized your divorce, chances are you are experiencing some relief. The stress and frustration of this oftentimes lengthy and difficult process are over!

However, just because you are done with the divorce process doesn't mean that all of your hardships magically disappear. Divorce is an adjustment, and you might find yourself wondering, "What's next?" You might suddenly find yourself coping with single parenthood. You might be adjusting to life in a new house or apartment. You might find that you need to go back to school or work in order to support yourself. Because divorce brings so many personal and professional changes, I'd like to devote this chapter to strategies for moving on after divorce.

Moving On Personally

"What's in a name?" Juliet muses in Shakespeare's *Romeo and Juliet.* As a recently divorced woman, you might give this question a lot of thought. There's no doubt that you are the same person whether you keep your ex-husband's name or not, but a name can symbolize your life choices. There is no right or wrong choice to make in this situation. This is a personal decision, and it is about doing what makes you the most comfortable. If you are not sure as to what you should do, consider the following pros and cons of keeping your married name.

One reason that divorced women keep their married name is that they feel comfortable with this name. If people in your neighborhood or at work know you by your married name, and you don't want that to change or go through the effort of correcting every person that calls you by this name, then keep your husband's last name. If you are anxious about correcting friends or acquaintances when they call you by your ex-husband's last name and you don't want to explain your divorce to them, it might be easier and less stressful to keep your married name. One other reason to keep your married name is that you will keep the same last name as your children. These are all good reasons to keep your ex-husband's last name.

On the other hand, if you feel as though your divorce has given you an opportunity for a fresh start, changing your last name makes sense. Changing your name to your maiden name will give you a clean break from your marriage and it can empower you to have confidence in your new identity. You might also want to consider your professional career when deciding if you should change your name. People in your field might recognize your maiden name, especially if you stopped working when you got married. If you think it will help people recognize you when you apply for jobs, changing your name back to your maiden name might be a good idea.

Even if you don't know if you want to change your name, you should check to see if you have the option to do so. In order to be able to change your name, your divorce decree has to include this option. If it doesn't, the name changing process will become difficult.

In order to legally change your last name, an amendment must be made to your divorce decree. Getting this done will require more court appearances and lawyer fees if you choose to hire counsel to help you through this process. It is a good idea to make sure that the name changing option is included in the divorce decree before your divorce is finalized to avoid this issue.

If your divorce decree does include the option to change your name, this process is simple. You won't have to fill out any additional paperwork or pay any extra fees. The only task required of you is to inform utility companies and other agencies of your change in name (for example, the DMV, the social security office, etc.).

Dating

Another aspect of life after divorce that can be difficult is dating. After your divorce, you might be hesitant to let potential partners into your life, given the hurt you experienced as a result of your divorce. It is perfectly normal to be nervous or intimidated by dating again. However, this fear or anxiety should not mean that your romantic life is over. Here are some tips to help you feel comfortable dating after your divorce.

Some people take years to get back on the dating scene after a divorce, while others jump into relationships right away. Once your divorce is finalized, it is a good idea to take some time to be single. After any breakup, you need some time to rediscover who you are and what you are looking for in a partner. To this end, you should explore your own interests, focus on your close friends and family, and reflect on your divorce.

If you have children, take time to help them heal from the divorce. Make sure that you remain close to them. Even if divorce was the right decision for you and your children, they are probably having a difficult time adjusting to their new routine. Before you begin spending time away from your kids while you date or introduce a new person into their lives, make sure they have time to heal from the divorce. You don't want to start dating again until you and your children have recovered from the divorce. Dating before you are ready can make this experience harder.

When you do feel that you are ready to start dating again, one low-pressure strategy is to go out with a group of friends. Being in a group of people can give you confidence and help you get used to meeting new people. When you are out with your friends, you can begin dating at your own pace. There isn't any pressure on you in this situation, as you can choose to stay with your friends when you go out places, or mingle more with other people that could be potential dates.

If you feel that you are ready to meet someone but aren't meeting the kind of person you'd want to date when you go out with your friends, you can try dating online. When you date online, you can find people who have the same interests and goals as you before you even go out with them. This way, you can be sure that you and the person you go out with have similar values and interests.

While it is important to take your time when getting back into the dating world, you also need to be prepared to get out of your comfort zone. Dating might feel foreign to you after being married for a long time, or you might be afraid of rejection, but don't let these fears hold you back. While it is always important to use your judgment in these situations, don't be afraid to take some risks.

Helping Your Children

Divorce means major changes for you and your entire family. For this reason, if you have kids, it is important to make sure that they are coping with the divorce in a healthy manner. As a parent, your instinct is to protect your children from hardships. While divorce can be a difficult time for children, it is by no means a scarring experience, particularly if you stay involved in your children's lives and pick up on clues that they are having a difficult time.

Many people fear that divorce has a negative effect on children. While this is true, it is important to keep in mind that this is the case because divorce is oftentimes a stressful event, and all stressful events have a negative effect on children.

For example, it is not uncommon for children's grades to drop and for them to experience a brief period of depression when they transition from one school to another. This is because moving to a new school disrupts their routines and increases their level of anxiety. But is the transition from middle to high school an emotionally scarring experience? Of course not! Children may initially be unhappy when they change schools, but this is not something that affects them for the rest of their lives.

Similarly, a divorce might have an initially negative effect on your children. However, once your kids acclimate to their new circumstances, they will most likely become happy once again and return to their normal lives. In fact, after the initial shock wears off, many children are even happier once their parents get divorced, especially if the kids experienced constant fighting and tension in their home while you were still married.

Another concern about divorce is that it will cause the children from the marriage to develop behavioral problems. Again, it is important to look at the facts when making statements like this. While divorce can increase children's risk of exhibiting psychological or behavioral problems, it does not cause these issues.

It is important that parents who recently went through a divorce are aware of the warning signs for these types of problems, but parents shouldn't assume that their children will exhibit these behaviors just because of the divorce. Parents can reduce the risk for behavioral problems by maintaining loving and open relationships with their children and getting them professional help if they do start to have behavioral issues.

It is easy to misinterpret data about children of divorced parents. Many parents overreact when, immediately after a divorce, their children begin acting out, seem depressed, or become uninterested in activities that they used to love. These behaviors will only be a problem if they persist for many months or years after the divorce. However, exhibiting these behaviors for a few weeks or months does not mean that your children are permanently scarred from the divorce.

While many children may experience some issues following divorce, these issues are not always long-term. But to be safe, it is important that you actively help your children recover from the divorce. This can be done by maintaining a stable home life for your children and showing them that you still love and care for them.

Visitation

Checking in with your child and taking care of them is simple enough if you have custody – but what about if you are sharing custody or have lost custody of your child? If you are not physically present in your child's life, you might feel as though your relationship has become strained. If you are estranged from your child because of your divorce, it is never too late to work on your relationship. Even if you have limited visitation or if you don't get along with your child's other parent, there are still ways that you can remain involved in your child's life.

One of the most important ways to continue building your relationship with your child, even after divorce, is by making them feel comfortable when you are together. While visitation is probably an awkward experience, especially in the beginning, do your best to make your meetings as fun and stress-free as possible.

To help make your child feel comfortable, it is important that you refrain from bad-mouthing your child's other parent. Never put your child in the middle of the issues you are having with your ex. Don't ask your child to pick sides or ask uncomfortable questions such as, "Don't you have more fun when you're with me?" or "You like me better, don't you?" These questions can do more harm than good and could alienate your child from you.

One issue that your child could have after divorce is wondering if you still love them. This is especially true for younger children, and it is a perfectly natural question to ask, especially if your child doesn't see you very often anymore.

In order to put these fears to rest, you need to make the effort to remain involved in your child's life. Depending on your situation, this can be achieved by attending special events, such as holidays, birthday parties, and sports games, or school events such as parent conferences and school plays. This will show your child that you are there for them and you want to celebrate their achievements.

Another way you can remain involved in your child's life and show them that you still care is by attending scheduled visitations regularly. Don't cancel these meetings or change them last minute. You need to give your child a sense of stability and routine, and this can be achieved by seeing them at regular, specific times. Even if you can only see your child a few days out of the month, check in with them regularly. This can be done by writing letters, connecting on social media, or making regular phone calls.

These tactics can be especially helpful if you have moved far away from your child. Thanks to modern technology, you can call, text, or Skype your child regularly and still remain involved in their life. By continuing a presence in your child's life, they will feel more comfortable with you and will adjust to the new living situation without much trouble.

If you are trying to reconnect with a teenager or an adult, you should still remain a presence in their life, but you should approach the situation slightly differently. Older children or adults will form their own opinions on your divorce, and forcing a relationship with a child of this age can make them more reluctant to engage with you. Because teenagers and adults will have their own opinions about the divorce, it is a good idea to be open and honest about the divorce with your child. Listen to their opinions, concerns, and fears. This can help both of you move past the divorce and maintain your relationship.

You should make it clear to your child that you are interested in continuing a strong relationship and you are willing to make time to meet or talk, but don't force a meeting until your child is ready. You should consistently make an effort to get in touch with your child, but be aware of the level of responsiveness that you get. If your child doesn't seem interested in meeting up, doesn't return your phone calls, or doesn't take the initiative to contact you, they might have leftover resentment from the divorce and might not be ready to reconnect with you. If this is the case, you might want to give your child some space for the time being.

Moving On Professionally

Going Back To School

After you get a divorce, your financial situation will probably change. This is especially the case if your spouse contributed to your family income, or if you were a stay-at-home parent while your spouse worked to pay the bills. While your family expenses will probably decrease because you are no longer supporting your spouse, you will have to find a way to support yourself and your children, if you have any. For some, this means getting a second job or looking for a job that pays more money. For others, it means going back to work altogether.

One way to make yourself more marketable if you are looking for a job that pays well is to go back to school. While this might seem like an expensive and timely option, in the long run it can certainly pay off. And if your ex is paying you rehabilitative alimony, you could get a degree with the help of your ex-spouse. This is an option that you should seriously consider if you find yourself in a position where you need to make more money.

There are many different reasons to enroll in an educational program. For example, maybe you're interested in getting a competitive edge in your job market. Or maybe you are interested in changing careers. You could even be interested in taking courses to explore new interests in life after divorce. Whatever the reason, many people who are recently divorced decide to go back to school. If this is something that you are interested in, you need to determine the right program for you.

There are degrees for all different levels of education. For example, if you did not finish high school, you can get a General Education Development (GED) certificate. This is the equivalent of a high school diploma. If you are trying to find a job and you don't have a high school diploma, there are not many options out there for you.

Getting your GED will make you more marketable and give you more options when applying for jobs. Obtaining your GED is fairly simple because you are not required to take a course. You just have to take a test and pass in five subjects: Reading, Writing, Science, Mathematics, and Social Studies. This is a quick, inexpensive way to increase your marketability as a potential employee.

If you finished high school but never finished college, maybe you want to enroll in a Bachelor's degree program. Especially in this day and age, a Bachelor's degree may assist in the job market. If you have been out-of-work for many years and you want to update your skill set, getting a Bachelor's degree can improve your resume and lead to better job possibilities. If you want to work part-time while you get your degree, this is possible through night classes or online classes. There are many different options to work around your schedule.

Unfortunately, in today's job market, having a Bachelor's degree is not always enough to set you apart from your competitors. For this reason, if you already have your undergraduate degree, you should look into getting a Master's degree. The Master's degree is becoming more and more common in today's job market. For some jobs, you must have a Master's degree in order to apply. Master's degrees in programs such as social work or nursing can greatly increase your earning potential.

Many people who decide to go back to school are concerned about how they will pay for it. It might seem counterintuitive to spend money in order to get a job. However, there are many ways to make the cost of higher education more affordable. For example, you can consider enrolling in a community college. This type of school has had increased enrollment in the past few years. As a result, many community colleges now offer four-year programs, and they do it for a fraction of the cost of traditional colleges.

You can always start your education at a community college and transfer credits to a more reputable college. This will save you money while you take core classes and make a traditional college experience more affordable. And again, if you received rehabilitative alimony from your spouse in your divorce, additional schooling will be more affordable.

Health Insurance

There are a few other business aspects that you should consider after you get a divorce. You will have to update your personal information, such as your health plan and your Will, because your ex-spouse will no longer be included in them. While some people decide to stay on a health coverage plan with their ex-spouse, there are other options that might be more suitable to your situation.

Because of divorce, some people lose their health coverage plan and get their own plan as a result. If this is your situation, you should consider your options for your new health coverage plan. While you should take some time to determine the best plan for you, you don't want to wait too long, because leaving your health and finances unprotected is never a good idea. If possible, you should be proactive and start working on your new health coverage plan before you stop using the one from your marriage.

Making sure that you have health coverage is essential, because without health benefits, trips to the doctor's office, hospital bills, and accidents can cost you thousands of dollars. You should always be prepared for the unexpected, and if something does happen, you need the peace of mind that a health coverage plan brings. While you are going through divorce, you can ask for health benefits as part of your settlement, depending on your situation. Generally, in situations where you and your spouse have children together, this is a potential option.

If you no longer receive health coverage after your divorce, you could get a new health plan through your job. While it can be expensive to get a health plan by yourself, this is always an option. You should consider factors such as the services that the health plan offers, premium costs, and the prescriptions that are covered. If you can meet the needs of your family through a health plan offered at work, this is a good option.

Another way that you can get health coverage is by keeping your Consolidated Omnibus Budget Reconciliation Act of 1985 (COBRA) coverage. Under COBRA, you can keep your health plan for up to three years. While this is ultimately a temporary solution, it can give you the time that you need to figure out a new plan. One drawback of COBRA is that you have to pay full premiums, meaning that the costs will be high. For this reason, you should only view COBRA as a temporary solution. When you get a new health coverage plan or if you remarry, the COBRA coverage will end.

If you find that you cannot afford a health plan because of your divorce, you can apply for government aid. One example of government aid is Medicaid. Another option is buying an individual health plan. Getting an individual health plan is the best option in some cases. While individual health plans can be high and the rates are usually based on your medical history, you can remove features to make the plan fit your lifestyle and be more affordable. Keep in mind that by picking a plan with a higher deductible, you will have lower monthly premiums. If no other options are available to you, getting an individual health plan is in your best interest.

Tax Changes

Just as married couples have specified taxes, so do people going through divorce. Many questions can arise concerning divorce and its tax consequences. Alimony and support are two big questions that arise when trying to deal with these issues. If you have recently undergone a divorce or are in the process of getting divorced, and you are unsure about how to file for taxes, you should talk to a lawyer.

Ideally, you would like to find a lawyer who has a strong finance background and a lot of experience dealing with situations similar to yours. Your lawyer should address the issues that you might face in the state of Connecticut. One of the many issues that you could face as a tax consequence of divorce in Connecticut is the question of alimony. Alimony is taxed to the recipient and deducted from the payer. Spousal support works in this way, with the recipient being taxes and the payer receiving the deductible.

Another tax issue deals with child dependency exemptions. In general, the spouse that has custody of the child or the one who truly needs the benefit will be exempt. Home mortgage interest is another issue because interest being paid on a mortgage can be deductible. You should take all of these possible deductions into consideration when doing your taxes and talk to an attorney or an accountant so that you can fully understand what you owe. It can also be difficult to determine how you file for taxes if you are separated or in the process of getting a divorce.

If you are in the process of getting a divorce and you are legally unmarried by the last day of the year, you cannot file for taxes as married. This means that timing your divorce and the tax year will be important if you are concerned about filing for taxes.

There are many aspects of tax consequences that go along with divorce. You should consider issues such as alimony and support when taxes come up. If you are on good terms with your former spouse, talk to them about any issues that you are having. A lawyer can always help you figure out what you owe and what you are entitled to receive.

Changing Your Will

In addition to changing your health coverage plan after divorce, you might want to look into updating your Last Will and Testament. Chances are that you included your spouse in your Will and Estate Plan when you were married. Now that you are no longer together, you may want to consider changing your Will and Estate Plan. In order to update your Will, it is in your best interest to contact an attorney. Your attorney can answer questions that you have about the process and help you through it. It is a good idea to update your Will after any major life event, so working with a lawyer every few years to update your Will is important.

When you get divorced, your family structure will change. This means that your ex-spouse might not be the only person you want to exclude from your Will. If you were planning on leaving assets to your spouse's family, for example their siblings or parents, you might change your mind about this after you get divorced. Changing your Will gives you the opportunity to reevaluate your assets and whom you want to give your assets to. Reevaluating your assets might also be prudent after divorce because divorce can change your property and assets.

Oftentimes in divorce, property is divided and assets are lost. On the other hand, divorce can mean acquiring new property or assets. If either of these is the case you should remove these assets from or add them to your Will. Another reason why it is a good idea to update your Will after divorce is because many people list their spouses as the executors of their Wills. If your ex-spouse is the executor of your Will, you will probably want to change this and name someone else as the executor.

There are a few different ways that you can change your Will. One way that you can add to your Will is through a Codicil to a Will. If you have many changes to make to your Will, you might find that it is best to start from scratch. If you feel that this is the case, you can write a new Will in order to make any necessary changes. Again, having a lawyer assist you with this process will make it much quicker and easier.

CONCLUSION

Thank you for taking the time to read my book. I hope that this book has answered your questions about the Connecticut divorce process and has put your fears to rest. While many people view divorce as a frightening and daunting process, once they get the facts and understand the divorce process, they feel much more confident and at ease.

If you still have questions, or if you feel that it is in your best interest to hire me to help you through your divorce, you can contact me. I would be happy to set up a consultation, in which we can determine if hiring me is the right choice for you. Please keep in mind that I can assist with other family law matters as well. Whatever your next step is, I wish you the best of luck in this process and beyond.

Please feel free to contact me if you have any questions. My phone number is 203-713-8877 and my email address is trd@consumerlegalservicesllc.com